AN INDEX TO ROADS SHOWN IN THE ALBEMARLE COUNTY

VIRGINIA

SURVEYORS BOOKS

1744–1853

Virginia Genealogical Society
Richmond, Virginia

Published with Permission from the

Virginia Transportation Research Council
(A Cooperative Organization Sponsored Jointly by
the Virginia Department of Transportation
and the University of Virginia)

HERITAGE BOOKS
2012

HERITAGE BOOKS
AN IMPRINT OF HERITAGE BOOKS, INC.

Books, CDs, and more—Worldwide

For our listing of thousands of titles see our website
at
www.HeritageBooks.com

Published 2012 by
HERITAGE BOOKS, INC.
Publishing Division
100 Railroad Ave. #104
Westminster, Maryland 21157

International Standard Book Numbers
Paperbound: 978-0-7884-3666-6
Clothbound: 978-0-7884-9214-3

AN INDEX TO ROADS SHOWN IN THE ALBEMARLE COUNTY SURVEYORS
BOOKS 1744-1853

by

Nathaniel Mason Pawlett

Faculty Research Historian

Virginia Highway & Transportation Research Council
(A Cooperative Organization Sponsored Jointly by the Virginia
Department of Highways & Transportation and the University of Virginia)

Charlottesville, Virginia

March 1976
Revised November 2003
VHTRC 76-R45

PREFACE

The Virginia Highway and Transportation Research Council is a co-operative organization sponsored jointly by the Virginia Department of Highways and Transportation and the University of Virginia and is located on the Grounds of the University at Charlottesville. The Council engages in a comprehensive program of research in the field of transportation. As a part of its program the Council, in December 1972, began research on the history of road and bridge building technology in Virginia. The initial effort was concerned with truss bridges; a complementary effort concentrating on roads got under way in October 1973.

The evolution of the road system of Virginia is in many ways inseparable from the social, political and technological developments that form the history of the Commonwealth. Despite this, there are few, extant serious works on the history of roads in Virginia. Those which have been produced focus on internal improvements and turnpike development before the War Between the States. Little has been done on the period from Reconstruction through the creation of the system of state highways in the earlier part of this century.

Accordingly, it was decided to investigate the development of the roads within a single county. Using this experience, a history of its roads would be produced as well as a procedural handbook for the writing of road histories. Due to the location of the Research Council, Albemarle County was chosen for this pilot study. The period chosen was 1725-1816. During the early stages of this project it was necessary to examine and extract all the road orders for the counties from which Albemarle was formed as well as the orders for Albemarle when it still contained the Counties of Amherst, Buckingham, Fluvanna, Nelson, and parts of Appomattox, Bedford and Campbell. The later road orders concerning Albemarle will ultimately be published with the road history, but the broad applicability of those for Goochland, Louisa and early Albemarle, and the opinions of various authorities throughout the state who examined them, indicated that they should have separate publication in order to make them generally available to individual scholars through libraries and educational institutions. Therefore, the first three publications of this series, *Louisa County Road Orders 1742-1748*, *Goochland County Road Orders 1728-1744* and *Albemarle County Road Orders 1744-1748*, were prepared, indexed and published.

In December 1974, a request was received from James A. Bear, Jr., Resident Director and Curator of the Thomas Jefferson Memorial Foundation at Monticello. Mr. Bear, engaged in editing Thomas Jefferson's Account Books for publication, wanted to know the original route of the Three Notch'd Road between Richmond and the Valley.

The report prepared for him elicited so much interest that it was ultimately expanded to include a folding map, the results of a reconnaissance by two Council members, an appendix of the pertinent information from the Order Books of Louisa, Goochland, Albemarle and Orange Counties, citations in the *Virginia Gazette* of Williamsburg, and photographs of portions of the road abandoned and still in service. Accordingly, this accumulated information was issued as the fourth publication of this series.

During the research at Albemarle County Court House three Surveyors Books covering the years 1744-1853 were discovered. The plats contained in these books showed many roads in present Albemarle County as well as Amherst, Buckingham, Fluvanna, Nelson, and parts of Appomattox, Bedford, and Campbell Counties which were at one time within it. Photographic copies were made of these plats, and after annotation an index was arranged to provide for easy reference as the remaining road orders of Albemarle County (1783-1816) were analysed and indexed. As the utility of this index came to be increasingly recognized it was decided to issue it as another publication in this series.

Note: This volume was slightly revised in 2003. The revisions primarily constituted changes in typeface and formatting in order to improve legibility, and did not include substantive changes to the text.

AN INDEX TO ROADS SHOWN IN THE
ALBEMARLE COUNTY SURVEYORS BOOKS 1744-1853

By

Nathaniel Mason Pawlett
Faculty Research Historian

Albemarle County, formed from Goochland in 1744, is fortunate in having preserved in its records three volumes of surveys made by the surveyors of the county between 1744 and 1853. In a sense, Albemarle County's good fortune extends to several other counties in central Virginia for they were at one time partially or wholly within the confines of the county (see below). These books therefore contain information of great value to those engaged in research on these counties. These additional counties and their periods of inclusion in these books are:

Amherst 1744-1761
Appomattox (portions) 1744-1761
Bedford (portions) 1744-1754
Buckingham 1744-1761
Campbell (portions) 1744-1754
Fluvanna 1744-1777
Nelson 1744-1761

Although indexed by names of patentees for whom the surveys were made these books contain a great deal of information not readily apparent from a perusal of the index. Owners of adjacent land locations of patents and grants and locations and names of roads of the colonial and early national period are apparent on many of them. The following index lists these roads, named as well as those still unidentified and the county within which they are presently located.

As previously stated, the Albemarle County Surveyors Books consist of three volumes. Two of these make up Book I, and the final volume by itself is Book II. This index has been arranged to reflect this fact. Roman numerals indicate the book number while the preceding digit, where used, refers to part 1 or part 2 of Book I. The number following the Roman numeral is the page number of the particular volume.

Spellings from the books are shown except in a few cases (Beard's, Barringer's) where the original name is at considerable variance with the current name. In these cases the original name is listed in parenthesis after the spelling used on the surveyor plat.

THE DEVELOPMENT OF ALBEMARLE COUNTY

Note: As originally published, this volume included maps showing the evolution of the county. These maps are not included in the revised and electronic versions due to legibility considerations. Instead, a verbal description is provided.

By the 1720s, the area that is now Albemarle County was part of the western reaches of Goochland County (created in 1728 from Henrico County) and Hanover County (created in 1721 from New Kent County). In 1742, the western section of Hanover was cut off as Louisa County (then including the northern third of modern-day Albemarle County).

Albemarle County was created in 1744 from Goochland County. In its original form, Albemarle contained the southern two-thirds of modern Albemarle County, the entirely of the modern counties of Amherst, Buckingham, Nelson, and Fluvanna, and parts of Appomattox, Campbell, and Bedford counties. Albemarle's boundaries were considerably reduced with the creation of Buckingham County (then also containing part of modern Appomattox County) and Amherst County (then also containing present-day Nelson County) in 1761. The year 1762 brought a slight northward expansion of the county boundaries, with the addition to Albemarle of the western portion of Louisa County. This brought Albemarle's western, southern, and northern boundaries to their current locations. With the last reduction in its territory, the creation of Fluvanna County in 1777, Albemarle reached its present size.

Index to Roads

Note: The modern county in which a road was located is noted in italics and brackets

Key:

(1)I = Plat Book I, part 1
(2)I = Plat Book I, part 2
II = Plat Book II

Key:

(1)I = Plat Book I, part 1
(2)I = Plat Book I, part 2
II = Plat Book II

Clark's Road *[Alb. Co.]*, **(2)I**, 87

Colemans Road *[Appo. Co.]*, **(1)I**, 154, 155

Coles Road *[Alb.-Fluv. Co.]*, **(2)I**, 126, 145; **II**, 32

Court House Road *[Alb.-Fluv. Co.]*, **(1)I**, 158, 315, 320; **(2)I**, 20

Court House Road *[Buck. Co.]*, **(1)I**, 41, 180, 253

Davises Thoroughfare *[Amherst-Nelson Co.?]*, **(1)I**, 129

Dutch Path *[Nelson Co.?]*, **(1)I**, 265

Ferry Road *[Alb. Co.]*, **(2)I**, 145

Ferry Road, *[Buck. Co.]*, 1I293

Road to Finley's Gap *[Alb. Co.]*, **(2)I**, 111

Fitzpatrick's Road *[Alb. Co.]*, **(1)I**, 306

Fluvanna Road *[Alb.-Fluv. Co.]*, **II**, 22

Fortunes Road *[Alb. Co.]*, **II**, 4

Glovers Road *[Buck. Co.]*, **(1)I**, 3, 5$^{(2)}$, 49, 87, 136, 246; **(2)I**, 2

Goodwins Road *[Nelson or Buck. Co.?]*, **(1)I**, 225, 282

Green Mountain Road *[Alb. Co.]*, **(1)I**, 314; **(2)I**, 160

Haden's Road *[Fluv. Co.]*, **(2)I**, 118

Hamner's Road *[Alb. Co.]*, **(2)I**, 136

Road to Hardware *[Alb. Co.]*, **(1)I**, 10

Mr. Harvie's Road *[Nelson Co.?]*, **(1)I**, 49

Road to Hendersons New Warehouse *[Alb. Co.]*, **(2)I**, 163

Doct. Hopkins's Road *[Fluv. Co.]*, **(2)I**,107

Saml. Hopkins Road *[Fluv. Co.]*, **(1)I**, 322

Hopkins Road *[Fluv. Co.]*, **(1)I**, 320, 322; **(2)I**, 5

Key:

(1)I = Plat Book I, part 1
(2)I = Plat Book I, part 2
II = Plat Book II

Horn Quarter Road *[Buck. Co.]*, **(2)I**, 1

Howards Road *[Buck. Co.]*, **(1)I**, 95, 225, 281

Irish Road *[Alb. Co.]*, **(1)I**, 309, 320, **(2)I**, 93, 110

Colo. Jeffersons Road *[Alb. Co.]*, **(1)I**, 321

Joplins Tract *[Alb. Co.]*, **(2)I**, 145

Martin King's Road *[Alb.-Fluv. Co.]*, **(1)I**, 50, 62, 194, 195, 196, 242, 310$^{(2)}$, 317, 319, 321; **(2)I**, 126, 127, 132, 160, 164; **II**, 3, 10, 22, 40

Road leading from the Store (Lindsays) *[Alb. Co.]*, **II**, 9

Main Louisa Road *[Alb. Co.]* **II**, 9

Lynches Road *[probably Appo. Co.]*, **(2)I**, 14

McCullough's Old Waggon Road *[Alb. Co.]*, **(2)I**, 105

McGehees Road *[Alb. Co.]*, **(2)I**, 120, 153, 163$^{(2)}$

Marrs Road *[Buck. Co.]*, **(1)I**, 293

Mazzies Road *[Alb. Co.]*, **(2)I**, 163

Mr. Megginsons Road *[Appo. Co.]*, **(1)I**, 236

Mill Stone Road *[probably Campbell Co.]*, **(1)I**, 181

Moon's road *[Alb. Co.]*, **(2)I**, 145, 146, 160, 162; **II**, 166

Mountain Road *[probably Alb. Co.]*, **(1)I**, 120; **(2)I**, 1

New Road *[Alb. Co.]*, **(2)I**, 120, 121$^{(2)}$

New Road *[Alb.-Fluv. Co.]*, **(2)I**, 126

New Road *[Fluv. Co.]*, **(2)I**, 121

Old Court Road *[Alb. Co.]*, **(2)I**, 120

Old Court House Road *[Alb. Co.]*, **(2)I**, 121, 145

Key:

(1)I = Plat Book I, part 1
(2)I = Plat Book I, part 2
II = Plat Book II

Old Court House Road *[Alb.-Fluv. Co.]*, **(2)I**, 126

Old Road *[Alb. Co.]*, **II,** 158, 192

Otter River Road *[Bedford-Campbell. Co.]*, **(1)I**, 186, 188

Road to Park Mills *[Alb. Co.]*, **II**, 151

Parson's New Road *[Alb. Co.]*, **(2)I**, 167

Paynes Road *[Alb.-Fluv. Co.]*, **(2)I**, 1

Piney Mountain Road *[Alb. Co.]*, **II**, 4$^{(2)}$

Ridge path *[Fluv. Co.]*, **(2)I**, 118

River Ridge Road *[Alb. Co.]*, **(2)I**, 111

Roads *[probably Alb. Co.]*, **(1)I**, 315; **(2)I**, 37, 45, 84, 86, 128$^{(2)}$, 130$^{(2)}$, 131, 133$^{(2)}$, 136, 139, 140$^{(3)}$, 141, 142, 144$^{(2)}$, 147$^{(2)}$, 149, 150$^{(3)}$, 151, 152, 153$^{(2)}$, 154, 155, 156, 157, 159, 164; **II**, 3$^{(2)}$, 6, 10, 17, 18, 22, 51, 55, 64, 73, 74, 75, 112, 143, 162, 172, 180, 182, 183, 191, 208

Roads *[Alb.-Fluv. Co.]*, **(1)I**, 155, 317; **(2)I**, 117

Roads *[Appo. Co.]*, **(1)I**, 139, 176, 189

Roads *[Buck Co.]*, **(1)I**, 40, 45, 48, 156, 183, 227, 238, 246, 300; **(2)I**, 2

Roads *[Fluv. Co.]*, **(1)I**, 31, 152; **(2)I**, 108

Roads [? Co.], **(1)I**, 136; **(2)I**, 38

Rock Fish Road *[Alb. Co.]*, **(1)I**, 260$^{(2)}$

Road to Rockfish Gap *[Alb. Co.]*, **(2)I**, 119, 165

Rockfish Gap Road *[Alb. Co.]*, **II**, 21

Key:

(1)I = Plat Book I, part 1
(2)I = Plat Book I, part 2
II = Plat Book II

Key:

(1)I = Plat Book I, part 1
(2)I = Plat Book I, part 2
II = Plat Book II

Woods's Old Road *[Alb. Co.]*, **(2)I**, 88

Road to Woods Gap *[Alb. Co.]*, **II**, 156

Road from Wood's Quarter to Charlottesville *[Alb. Co.]*, **(2)I**, 163

Woodsons Road *[Fluv. Co.]*, **(1)I**, 321, 322

Other Heritage Books by the Virginia Genealogical Society
Published with Permission from the Virginia Transportation Research Council
(A Cooperative Organization Sponsored Jointly by the Virginia Department of Transportation and the University of Virginia):

Other Heritage Books by the Virginia Genealogical Society: